WITHDRAWN

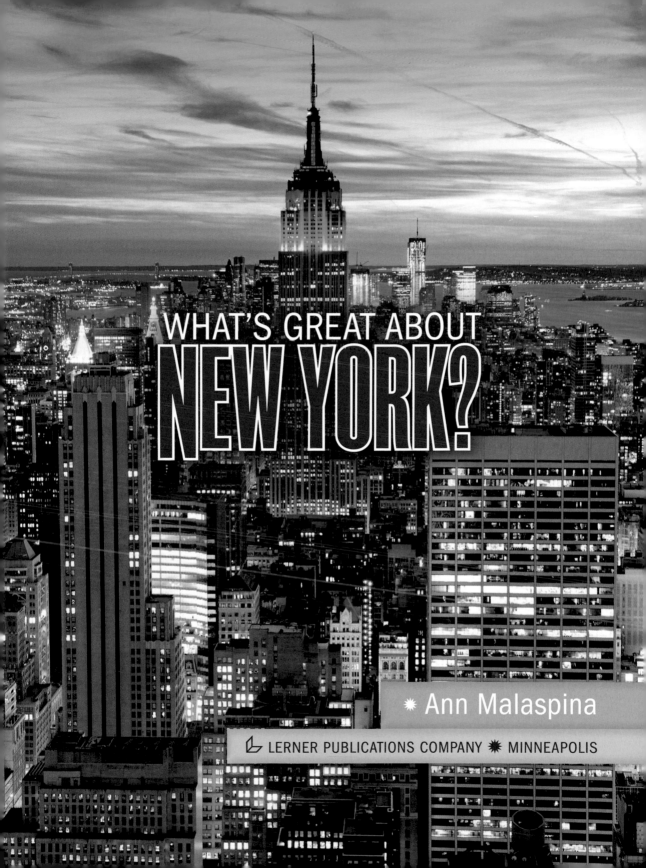

WHAT'S GREAT ABOUT
NEW YORK?

✳ Ann Malaspina

⌐ LERNER PUBLICATIONS COMPANY ✳ MINNEAPOLIS

CONTENTS

NEW YORK
WELCOMES YOU! * 4

Copyright © 2015
by Lerner Publishing Group, Inc.

Content Consultant: Harriet Alonso, Professor
of History, The City College of New York

All rights reserved. International copyright
secured. No part of this book may be
reproduced, stored in a retrieval system, or
transmitted in any form or by any means—
electronic, mechanical, photocopying,
recording, or otherwise—without the prior
written permission of Lerner Publishing
Group, Inc., except for the inclusion of brief
quotations in an acknowledged review.

Lerner Publications Company
A division of Lerner Publishing Group, Inc.
241 First Avenue North
Minneapolis, MN 55401 USA

For reading levels and more information, look
up this title at www.lernerbooks.com.

Main body text set in ITC Franklin Gothic Std
Book Condensed 12/15.
Typeface provided by Adobe Systems.

Library of Congress Cataloging-in-Publication
Data

Malaspina, Ann, 1957–
      What's great about New York? / by Ann
Malaspina.
          pages   cm. — (Our great states)
      Includes index.
      ISBN 978-1-4677-3335-9 (lib. bdg. :
      alk. paper)
      ISBN 978-1-4677-4714-1 (eBook)
      1. New York (State)—Juvenile literature.
   2. New York (State)—History—Juvenile
   literature. I. Title.
   F119.3.M164 2015
   974.7—dc23   2013043721

Manufactured in the United States of America
1 - PC - 7/15/14

NEW YORK Welcomes You!

"I Love New York" is a perfect song for a great state. New York has something for everyone. You can hike a trail in the Catskill Mountains or ride the subway in Manhattan. Or you might want to explore Central Park. The Adirondack Mountains are a peaceful place to visit. You may prefer the noise and lights on Broadway. Read on to discover ten things that make New York great. Soon you may even be planning a visit!

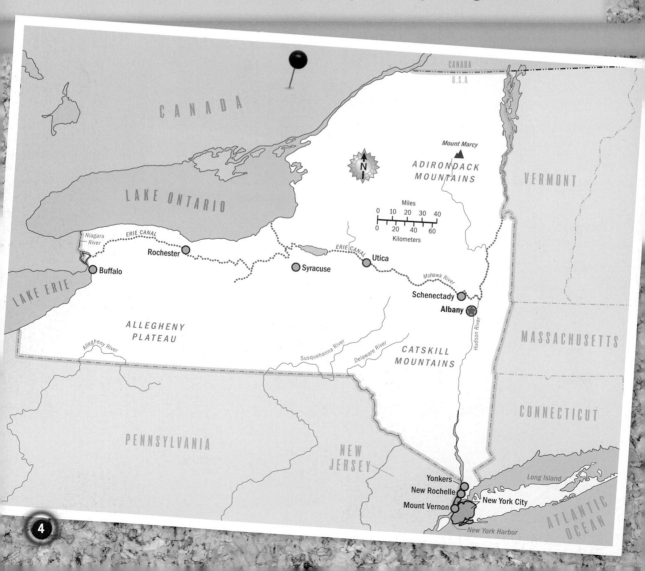

WELCOME TO NEW YORK

The Empire State

Explore New York's famous landmarks and all the places in between! Just turn the page to find out all about the EMPIRE STATE. >

THE BIG APPLE

> More than 8.3 million people live in New York City. Many come to follow their dreams. Actors try out for Broadway shows. Authors hope to write a best-selling book.

The Empire State Building is a popular sight to see. Climb 1,575 steps to the 86th-floor observatory. Or take a quick elevator ride. You can see Pennsylvania on a clear day from this height. The Empire State Building opened in 1931. It was the tallest building in the world then. It stands 1,250 feet (381 meters) tall. The record for racing up the stairs to the 86th floor is nine minutes, thirty-three seconds. It was set in 2003. How fast could you make it to the 86th floor?

End your day relaxing at Central Park. It is the city's 843-acre (341-hectare) green oasis. There are seven bodies of water in the park. Rent a rowboat. Horseback riding, skating, and fishing are also fun.

North of Central Park is Harlem. This is a historic African American neighborhood. Singers and dancers try out for Amateur Night at the Apollo Theater. They hope to become famous.

The Apollo Theater is one of the oldest music halls in New York City.

APOLLO
The Soul of American Culture
TOUR THE APOLLO THEATER
On Sale Now

The Empire State Building rises high above the city.

FIRST CAPITAL

> New York City was the first capital of the United States. George Washington became president on April 30, 1789. He took the oath of office at Federal Hall. You can stand where Washington stood! The capital later moved to Philadelphia, Pennsylvania, and then to Washington, DC.

New Yorkers wanted to honor George Washington. They named a bridge built between Manhattan and New Jersey after him. The George Washington Bridge over the Hudson River opened in 1931. Take a bike ride over the bridge during your visit.

The Brooklyn Bridge was a wonder when it opened in 1883. It was the longest suspension bridge in the world. It was also very strong. Circus owner P. T. Barnum led camels and elephants across the bridge. This showed the bridge's strength. People cheered for Jumbo the elephant. You can take the same walk!

People in the 1880s were amazed by the Brooklyn Bridge.

ALBANY

New York City is the largest city in the state. But it is not the capital. Would you like to see where the governor works? You'll need to travel approximately 135 miles (217 kilometers) north to Albany. Catch a train at Penn Station in New York City. You'll be in Albany in less than three hours.

ON THIS SITE IN FEDERAL HALL
APRIL 30 1789
GEORGE WASHINGTON
TOOK THE OATH AS THE FIRST PRESIDENT
OF THE UNITED STATES
OF AMERICA

Musicians share their talents in the subway stations.

SUBWAYS

> Hop on the subway! It is the best way to get around New York City. The subway system first opened in 1904. It has about 722 miles (1,162 km) of tracks. Most of the tracks are belowground. The city needs 6,311 cars to carry 1.7 billion riders each year. Subways run twenty-four hours a day, seven days a week.

Artists decorate subway stations with figures, paintings, and colorful tiles. Street musicians play in the busiest stations. Poems are posted on subway cars. Even belowground, New Yorkers love the arts.

You can ride the subway all day. Take the A train if you want a long ride. It travels more than 31 miles (50 km) each way. The ride begins at 207th Street in Manhattan. It ends in Queens.

The New York City subway system has 468 stations in operation.

ON BROADWAY

> The marquees are lit up. The curtains are ready to rise. It's Saturday night on Broadway. Magic is in the air.

Do you prefer comedies, musicals, or dramas? You can take your pick on Broadway. Crowds pack the forty theaters around Broadway and 42nd Street most nights. You can see new shows or familiar favorites. Famous actors and rising stars pour their hearts out onstage.

Broadway is not just about the actors. The costume designers turn cloth into costumes. The musicians play songs to make us anticipate scenes. Or they might make us laugh or cry. The makeup artists change an actor into a ghost or a rock star. From your seat you might see dancing lions and zebras. They look real, but are they?

You can wait at the stage door after a show. You may get to meet your favorite actors. Have your program ready for an autograph.

The Lion King is one of Broadway's longest-running shows.

LADY LIBERTY

> Catch a boat to the Statue of Liberty at Battery Park. The statue is on Liberty Island in New York Harbor. France gave Lady Liberty to the United States in 1886.

Park rangers lead tours on Liberty Island. They also answer questions about the statue. Walk 215 steps into the statue's base. The Liberty Island Museum is here. You can learn about the statue's history. You can climb to the statue's crown if you're feeling adventurous. It is 377 steps from the lobby to the crown. There is no elevator!

A short boat ride away is Ellis Island. More than twelve million immigrants entered the United States here. They came from 1892 to 1954. You can follow the steps immigrants took one hundred years ago.

LADY LIBERTY'S POET

Emma Lazarus wrote a poem in 1883 that helped raise money for Lady Liberty's base. The Statue of Liberty was a sign of immigration and opportunity. Read the poem on the statue's base at the Statue of Liberty.

Visitors to the Statue of Liberty can climb up to her crown.

At Ellis Island, visitors can see what it was like for immigrants entering the United States.

9/11 MEMORIAL

The new One World Trade Center sits above the memorial.

> Terrorists attacked the United States on September 11, 2001. Visitors from around the world come to honor the victims of 9/11. They visit the National September 11 Memorial & Museum. They pay their respects to firefighters, first responders, and other heroes. These people lost their lives helping others on 9/11.

Two pools lie where the World Trade Centers once stood. Panels surround the pools. The names of the approximately three thousand people who died are on these panels.

Visit the Memorial Museum. It has photographs, videos, and objects to help visitors better understand 9/11. Rising above the memorial is a building called One World Trade Center. Its spire reaches 1,776 feet (541 m) into the sky. The number 1776 represents the year Americans declared their independence.

HUDSON RIVER

> The Hudson River starts in the Adirondack Mountains. It flows for 315 miles (507 km) down eastern New York. It passes through the Catskill Mountains and into New York Harbor. Here it empties into the Atlantic Ocean.

People kayak on the Hudson River and picnic in parks. Summertime concerts take place in some parks. You can visit Walkway Over the Hudson for a scenic view of the Hudson River. This state park is on an old railroad bridge. You can even take a swim at some points along the river.

If you pedal the Hudson River Park Bikeway in Manhattan, you may spot a tugboat pushing a barge. Barges share the river with passenger boats, sailboats, and cruise ships. Police boats, fireboats, and even stand-up paddleboards also share the river. Every September, tugboats line up to race on the Hudson River for the Annual Tugboat Race. They go fast!

THE *HALF MOON*

English explorer Henry Hudson sailed up the Hudson River in 1609. He was looking for a way to China and India. His ship was called the *Half Moon*. Hudson got as far as Albany. You can climb on a copy of the *Half Moon*. It's a traveling museum. It has traveled as far as North Carolina.

There are many great places to bike along the Hudson River.

ERIE CANAL

> It was big news when the Erie Canal opened in 1825. New York Harbor became a booming port. The 363-mile (584-km) waterway joins Lake Erie to the Hudson River in Albany.

In the early days, mules and horses pulled boats down the Erie Canal. Now, public towing and shipping takes place. People ride bikes and take hikes along the Erie Canalway Trail. There's a lot to discover along the waterway.

Take a ride on a small cruise boat. Watch the captain guide the ship through the lock. Invite your family to sleep on a houseboat. You may want to pitch a tent at a campsite by a waterway lock.

Remember to stay under the speed limit if you're canoeing. It's 10 miles (16 km) an hour!

Tugboats (*above*) must guide through locks (*below*) along the Erie Canal.

NIAGARA FALLS

> The huge falls on the Niagara River cross the border between the United States and Canada. The American Falls and the smaller Bridal Veil Falls are on the US side. The Horseshoe Falls are on the Canadian side. Together they are known as Niagara Falls.

You can hike the footpaths in Niagara Falls State Park. Or take a trolley tour through the park.

The Maid of the Mist boats have been running for more than 150 years. These boats take people close to the base of the Horseshoe Falls. Wear a raincoat, or you'll get soaked. You can also ride an elevator into the Niagara Gorge. Here you'll stand on the Hurricane Deck. It is just a few feet from the Bridal Veil Falls. Cars and walkers also cross the Rainbow Bridge over the gorge. Keep your eyes open for a rainbow in the mist.

Niagara Falls isn't just a natural wonder. It is also an important source of hydroelectric power. It provides power for millions of people in the United States and Canada.

YOUR TOP TEN!

It's time for you to write your New York Top Ten List. What would you like to see when you visit New York? What would you be most excited to visit if you were planning a New York vacation? These are questions to consider as you create your own top ten list. So grab a sheet of paper and a pencil, and get creative. If you'd like, you can even turn your list into a book and illustrate it with drawings or with pictures from the Internet or magazines.

The Maid of the Mist boats take you close to the falls.

Visitors can see the Bridal Veil Falls on the US side.

MAID OF THE MIST V

NEW YORK BY MAP

> MAP KEY

- ⬤ Capital city
- ⬤ City
- ⬤ Point of interest
- ▲ Highest elevation
- —··— International border
- —·— State border
- ······ Canal

Visit www.lerneresource.com to learn more about the state flag of New York.

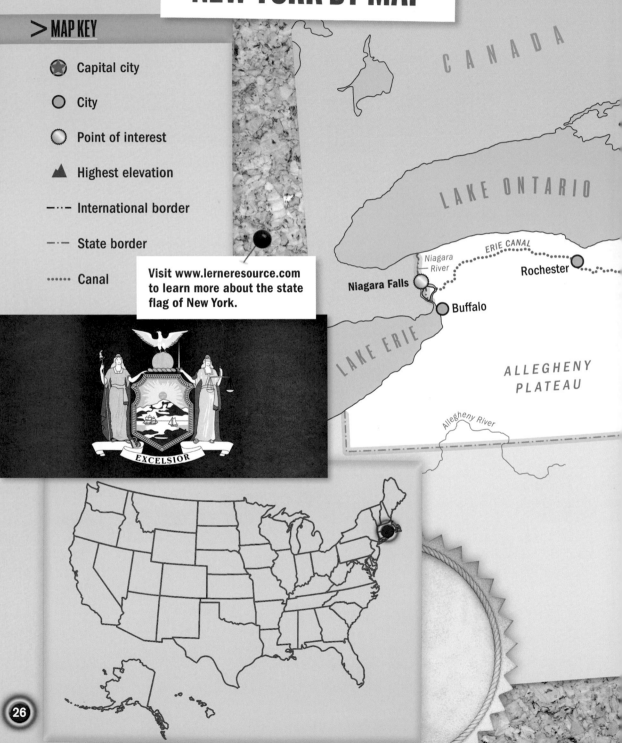

CANADA

LAKE ONTARIO

ERIE CANAL

Niagara River

Niagara Falls

Rochester

Buffalo

LAKE ERIE

ALLEGHENY PLATEAU

Allegheny River

EXCELSIOR

CANADA

U.S.A.

VERMONT

Mount Marcy
(5,343 feet/1,629 m)

ADIRONDACK
MOUNTAINS

N

Miles
0 10 20 30 40
0   20   40   60
Kilometers

ERIE CANAL
Utica

Syracuse

Mohawk River

Schenectady

Albany

Baseball Hall
of Fame
(Cooperstown)

Susquehanna River

Delaware River

CATSKILL
MOUNTAINS

Hudson River

MASSACHUSETTS

CONNECTICUT

- Empire State Building
- Central Park
- Apollo Theater
- Broadway
- 9/11 Memorial
- Federal Hall National Memorial

PENNSYLVANIA

NEW
JERSEY

Yonkers

New Rochelle

New York City

Mount Vernon

Statue of Liberty

New York Harbor

Long Island

ATLANTIC
OCEAN

NEW YORK FACTS

NICKNAME: Empire State

SONG: "I Love New York" by Steve Karmen

MOTTO: *Excelsior*, or "Ever Upward"

FLOWER: rose

> **TREE:** sugar maple

BIRD: eastern bluebird

> **ANIMALS:** beaver, brook trout, ladybug

FOOD: apple

DATE AND RANK OF STATEHOOD: July 26, 1788; the 11th state

> **CAPITAL:** Albany

AREA: 49,112 square miles (127,199 sq. km)

AVERAGE JANUARY TEMPERATURE: 32°F (0°C)

AVERAGE JULY TEMPERATURE: 77°F (25°C)

POPULATION AND RANK: 19,570,261; 3rd (2012)

MAJOR CITIES AND POPULATIONS: New York City (8,336,697), Buffalo (259,384), Rochester (210,532), Syracuse (144,170), Albany (97,904)

NUMBER OF US CONGRESS MEMBERS: 27 representatives, 2 senators

NUMBER OF ELECTORAL VOTES: 29

> **NATURAL RESOURCES:** timber, garnet, Herkimer diamonds, natural gas, petroleum

AGRICULTURAL PRODUCTS: milk, meat, poultry, apples, grapes, tart cherries, cabbage, sweet corn, onions, maple syrup

MANUFACTURED GOODS: chemicals, machinery, computer and other electronic products

STATE HOLIDAYS AND CELEBRATIONS: Brooklyn-Queens Day

GLOSSARY

amateur: a person who participates in an activity without payment

autograph: a person's signature written by hand

hydroelectric power: the energy generated by the pressure of falling water

immigrant: a person who travels to a country to live there

lock: an enclosure with gates at each end used to raise and lower boats

marquee: the sign over the entrance of a theater with the name of the show or movie

memorabilia: items collected because of their relationship to a particular interest

oasis: a place of peace

oath: a promise about one's future actions

observatory: a place providing a wide view

spire: a tall, pointed tower

suspension bridge: a bridge with a roadway suspended from cables that pass over towers and are strongly anchored at the ends

tugboat: a strongly built boat used for towing and pushing ships

LERNER

SOURCE

Expand learning beyond the printed book. Download free, complementary educational resources for this book from our website, www.lernerresource.com.

FURTHER INFORMATION

Brown, Don. *America Is Under Attack: September 11, 2001; The Day the Towers Fell*. New York: Flash Point, 2011. Find out more about the story of September 11, 2001, and the people whose lives were changed on that day.

Bullard, Lisa. *The Erie Canal*. Minneapolis: Lerner Publications, 2011. An engineering miracle, the Erie Canal opened up the West to settlers and commerce. The site comes alive with vibrant photos in this book.

National Baseball Hall of Fame and Museum
http://baseballhall.org
Find out about your favorite baseball players at the National Baseball Hall of Fame and Museum website. You can find biographies, videos, and photographs here.

New York State Department of State Kid's Room
http://www.dos.ny.gov/kids_room
Learn about New York State history, state symbols, and fun things to do in the Empire State.

Shea, Pegi Deitz. *Liberty Rising: The Story of the Statue of Liberty*. New York: Square Fish, 2013. A beautifully illustrated history of the building of the Statue of Liberty, this book explores the people behind the statue and how they created the monument.

Where's Waldo in New York?
http://www.nycgo.com/waldo
Before you visit the Big Apple, check out the official kids' guide to New York City. You'll find a lot of fun things to do and places to see, from parks to museums.

INDEX

PHOTO ACKNOWLEDGMENTS

The images in this book are used with the permission of: © Songquan Deng/ iStockphoto, p. 1; © littleny/Shutterstock Images, pp. 4, 7 (top), 10, 11, 16–17; © dibrova/Shutterstock Images, pp. 4–5; © Lerner Publications, pp. 5, 26–27, 26 (bottom); © Songquan Deng/Shutterstock Images, pp. 6–7; © Jose Fuste Raga/Corbis, pp. 7 (bottom), 8–9; Library of Congress, p. 8 (LC-USZ62–97318), p. 23 (top) (LC-DIG-ggbain-32385); © spirit of america/ Shutterstock Images, p. 9; © Sven Hoppe/ dpa/Corbis, pp. 10–11; © Tim Clayton/ Corbis, pp. 12–13; © ValeStock/ Shutterstock Images, p. 13; © Richard Cavalleri/Shutterstock Images, pp. 14–15; The New York Historical Society, p. 14; © Johnér Images/Corbis, p. 15; © Ben Cooper/Science Faction/Corbis, p. 16; © Zack Seckler/Corbis, pp. 18–19; Edward R. Shaw, p. 18; © scarletsails/iStockphoto, p. 19; © Debra Millet/Shutterstock Images, pp. 20–21; © Sean Donohue Photo/ Shutterstock Images, p. 21 (top); © Joseph Sohm/Visions of America/Corbis, p. 21 (bottom); © Nik Wheeler/Corbis, pp. 22–23; Bob Sandberg/Library of Congress, p. 23 (bottom); © Thomas Sbampato/ imagebroker/Corbis, p. 24–25; © Ritu Manoj Jethani/Shutterstock Images, p. 25 (top); © alexpro9500/Shutterstock Images, p. 25 (bottom); © nicoolay/iStockphoto, p. 26 (top); © epantha/iStockphoto, p. 29 (top); © kwiktor/iStockphoto, p. 29 (middle top); © Pete Spiro/Shutterstock Images, p. 29 (middle bottom); © Ivan Mateev/ iStockphoto, p. 29 (bottom).

Cover: © iStockphoto.com/JVT (Statue of Liberty); © iStockphoto.com/Aivolie (Niagara Falls); © Songquan Deng/ Shutterstock.com (NYC Skyline, Central Park); © Laura Westlund/Independent Picture Service (map); © iStockphoto.com/ fpm (seal); © iStockphoto.com/vicm (pushpins); © iStockphoto.com/benz190 (corkboard).